Published in the United States of America by The Child's World®
PO Box 326 • Chanhassen, MN 55317-0326
800-599-READ • www.childsworld.com

My First Steps to Math™ is a registered trademark of Scholastic, Inc.

Library of Congress Cataloging-in-Publication Data
Moncure, Jane Belk.
My seven book / by Jane Belk Moncure.
    p. cm. — (My first steps to math)
ISBN 1-59296-662-4 (lib. bdg. : alk. paper)
1. Counting—Juvenile literature. 2. Number concept—Juvenile literature. I. Title.
QA113.M667 2006
513.2'11—dc22
                        2005025697

My seven Book

by Jane Belk Moncure
illustrated by Ben Mahan

This is Little  seven .

Little  lives in the house of seven.

It has seven rooms. Count them.

Every day, Little  goes for a walk.

One day he walks by a pond.

He sees one big duck . . .

and six
little ducks.

How many ducks in all?

Some ducks say, *Quack, quack, quack.*

Some ducks dive under the water.
They are looking for snails.

Can you count how many heads
and how many tails?

Next, Little  sees frogs on a log.

He counts four . . .

and three
more.

How many frogs in all?

Little  claps seven claps. Can you?

How many frogs dive into the water?
How many frogs stay on the log?

Little  walks past the pond.

He comes to a big stump.

He sees a mama turtle and lots of little turtles. Count them.

Little  finds a net.

He catches the little turtles.

How many did he catch?
How many turtles are left?

The little turtles are sad. So Little  lets them go home to their mama.

Now count the happy turtles.

Next Little  sees a big mound of sticks.

"I will sit and rest," he says.

But a beaver peeks its head out.
"You are sitting on my house," it says.

15

Little  jumps away. Out come

two big
beavers . . .

and five little beavers. How many beavers are in the whole family?

"Watch us play," they say.

Little  seven says, "I will play, too."

He jumps seven times. Can you?
Guess what he finds.

He finds a big sandbox with a toy train in it.

How many cars is the engine pulling?

Little  builds a track for the train.

Then he makes a tunnel.

"I will pull the seven cars
through the tunnel," he says.

Little  pulls. Does the whole train come through the tunnel?

"It is getting late. I must go home," says Little seven.

On his way home, Little  sees some pennies.

How many coins does he find in all?

Little  hops to a

shop.

He looks in the window.
He sees lots of lollipops.

Little  sees a sign that says:

Lollipops 1 penny each .

"Whee!" says Little seven .

"I can buy lots of lollipops.
I have seven pennies."

How many lollipops can he buy?

He buys three cherry lollipops

and four grape lollipops.

Little seven eats two lollipops.

How many does he leave for you?

Little  finds seven of everything.

seven ducks   seven turtles

seven beavers

seven train cars

seven lollipops

Now you find seven things.

Let's add with Little 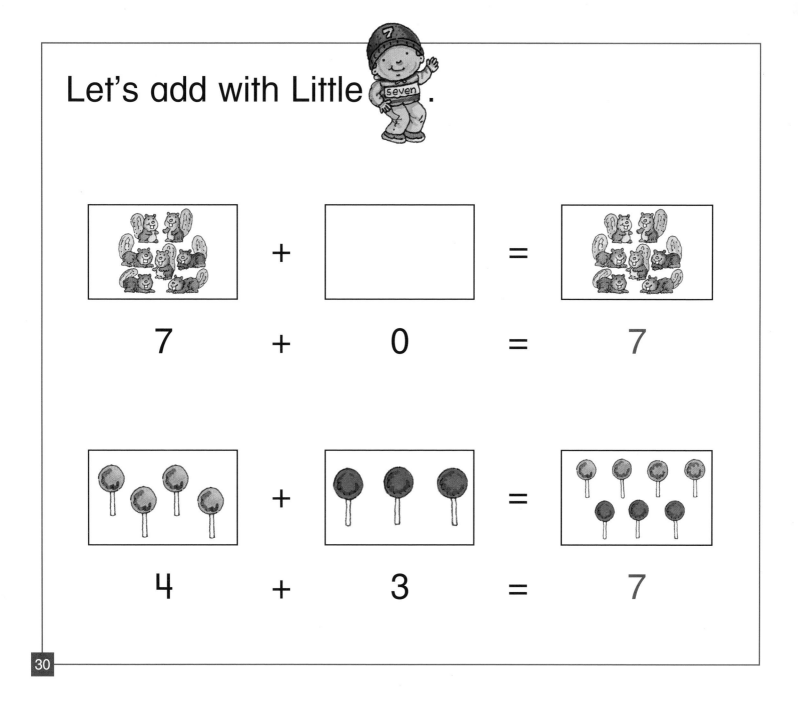seven.

7   +   0   =   7

4   +   3   =   7

Now take away.

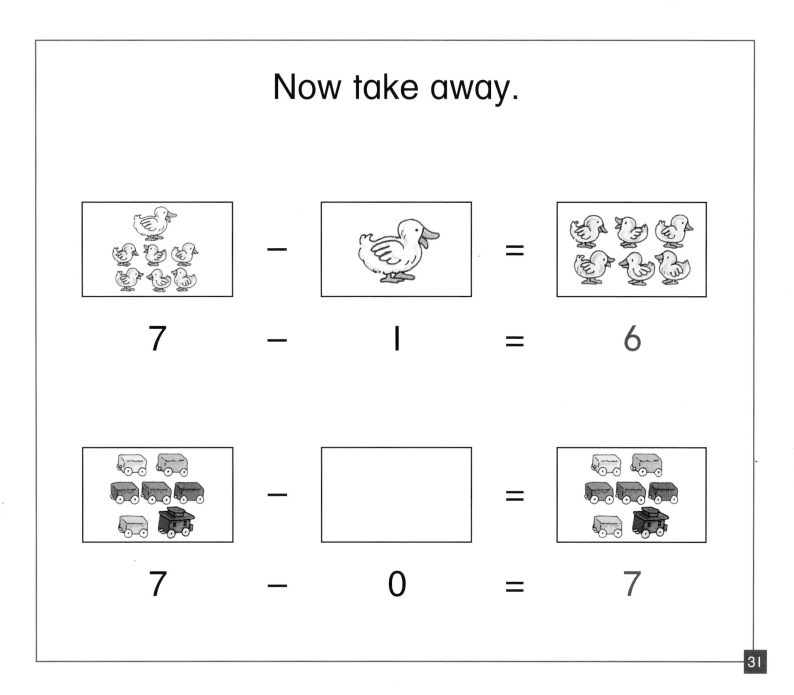

7   –   1   =   6

7   –   0   =   7

Little  seven makes a 7 this way:

7

He makes the number word like this:

seven

You can make them in the air with your finger.